Stewart's Creek

(The end of an era)

———————

By H Wayne Easter

i

Preface

Our home was in the foothills of the Blue Ridge Mountains: a half-mile west of Stewart's Creek in Surry County N C. We had no close neighbors and no one cared who roamed where in the huge backwoods. One wooded area beyond Little Sid Marshall's home had no owner; we called it "No Man's Land."

With arrowheads in the creek bottoms, tangled laurel bluffs to climb in, wild animal dens and deep dark fishing holes, Stewart's Creek became my favorite place to be. Nowhere else could I spend a whole day alone, fishing, wading and panning for gold.

I moved away in the 1950s; knowing my creek would always be there when I went back and so it was until 1970, when news came of a flood control dam to be built near Dave Carson's bottoms. The lake water would back up to the North Carolina-Virginia state line: covering exactly my favorite part of Stewart's Creek.

On a February Sunday in 1971, my son Mike and I made the following photos of some of the areas that were going underwater. With the foot logs of other years long gone, the creek too cold to wade and a rocky bluff too icy to climb, we didn't go below the Spruce Pine Hole. (As is always the case when it's far too late, I now wish we had.)

With four exceptions, all of the following photos were made that February day. When the two at the dam-site were made a year later, (in 1972) all of the best fishing holes had already been bulldozed. The Line Hole photo was made thirty-eight years later in 2009 and the final photo (of Watershed Lake) was made in 2002.

iii

Stewart's Creek

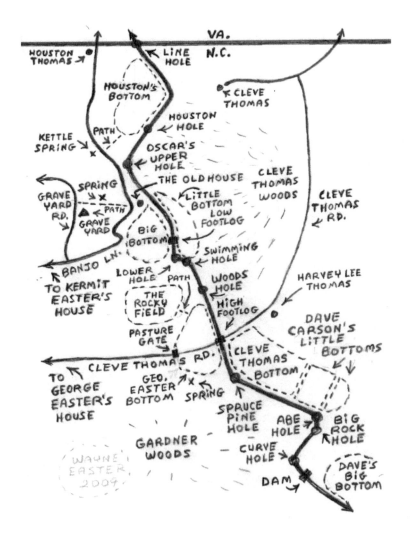

Stewart's Creek

The Cleve Thomas Road

Our trip began on the Cleve Thomas Road between the homes of my grandfather (George Washington Easter) and Grover Cleveland Thomas, who lived beyond the creek. The area shown above was a quarter mile west of the creek, looking back up the valley toward Grandpa's home and it went under water when the dam was built.

The hillside at right was once Grandpa's pasture and his cow wore a bell that could be heard when walking along the road. A row of faded white telephone poles with green-glass insulators still stood beside the road in the late 1930s: all that remained of a hand-cranked party line phone system once shared by neighbors.

Some gallon-sized rocks had rolled downhill into the road from a rocky cornfield on the hilltop. (Two budding scientists had checked out the theory of gravity and sure enough, every single one rolled downhill.) Lucky for us, nobody had got hurt; if they had, there would've been "you-know-what to pay" and some major hide loss for two boys.

Pa practiced his English language studies while plowing in rocky fields and he was especially good at French. I could almost see blue smoke in the air as the plow clanged along in the the rocks.

1

When crows pulled up new corn plants in spring, he shot one and hung it from a tall pole to scare other crows away. If that failed, he went to Plan B and set a steel trap on top of the pole. When a crow landed in the trap, it made such so much noise every other crow in the country flew in to see what was wrong. Then together, they made so much noise, everybody in the country knew Pa had caught another crow.

When a fertilizer dealer came by one day, Pa asked him about some of our pest problems. He told Pa, more or less, "I'm sure there are sufficient insecticides available to remedy your situation at small expense." I'd never heard such big words and I don't think Pa had either.

Dumb bull

When he was a young man, Pa made a dumb bull from a length of hollow log: with a banjo head cover stretched tightly over one end. He fastened a heavy wax-coated string to the inside of the cover and as he said it, "When you reached in there and slid your fingers along that string, it made a racket like nothin' you ain't never seen before."

He was walking along the Cleve Thomas Road one day and heard some people talking up on Gardner's Ridge. According to him, they had sneaked in breaking ivy. (A small green-all-year bush we gathered late in the year to make some extra money.)

We broke six-inch pieces from the bushes, strung them into fifty-foot lengths and sold them the T N Woodruff Company at Low Gap. They then sold them to cities nationwide to use for Christmas decorations.

No landowner cared who broke his ivy, but Pa, having nothing better to do, saw a chance to try out his new toy. When he heard the people, he ran home, got the dumb bull, hurried along Gardner's Ridge and sneaked up behind some bushes where two strangers were happily breaking ivy.

Again, as he told it, "I reached in there and give that string a dry yank and one of 'em said, "Listen!" I give 'er another harder yank and all Hell broke loose."

"Ivy sacks be-damned, they climbed all over the ivy bushes and each other and dived straight down through the bluff. They run straight across the branch and the Cleve Thomas Road and straight up through the cow pasture. I kept thrashin' the bushes and pullin' that string and last I seen, they was a' headin' outta' sight towards Lambsburg, might near too skeered to look back." (After hearing his tale, I was almost afraid to go anywhere near the place.)

Mike at Grandpa's bottom.

Grandpa's bottom was just beyond a drawbar pasture gate on the Cleve Thomas Road. Hundreds of water-worn creek rocks grew in a small area at the upper side and more came up after every rain. A pile of rocks got bigger every year, but there were so many, it was impossible to keep them picked up.

We were told, "You all stay outta' that rock pile; they's copperheads in there bigger'n you are." (I sat on the rock pile, ate the black berries that grew there and saw no snakes.)

3

The sun was just coming up as we walked barefoot along the Cleve Thomas Road to hoe corn in Grandpa's bottom. (One of five different bottoms we sharecropped at different times on Stewart's Creek.) We chopped weeds, hoed dirt and sweated blood all day long, as Pa plowed with a five-point cultivator and Old John. (The way he told it, he "follered the south end of a horse headed north from sun up to sundown.")

As the day got hotter, the long rows got longer and reached from one end to the other. All the while, Stewart's Creek sang a fishing song as it splashed down over the rapids at the Spruce Pine Hole. It might as well have been in another county, because there would be no fishing or wading on hoeing day.

We didn't need a water jug in the bottom, because of a cold spring that came from under a huge rock up in the bluff. When we took a break, we drank the spring dry, cooled our feet in the spring branch and "rested our weary bones" in the shade of some poplar trees.

The bluff at Grandpa's bottom

The mile-long bluff began downstream at the Curve Hole: a quarter mile below the Spruce Pine Hole, ran along beside Grandpa's Bottom and on to the Tom Hawks Woods far up the valley. The only break in the jungle was Grandpa's road that led uphill from his house to Lambsburg Road. In "big bloom years," the bluff was a mile-long ocean of laurel blooms.

4

The tangled bluff was almost impossible to climb through and just made for scouts and hunters like me. Pa's take on the subject, "Ain't nobody but a' idiot messes around in there, boy," (I could see forever from my lookout tree halfway up the bluff and best of all, nobody could see me.)

An imported blight began killing the native chestnut trees in New York City and slowly spread south. It came to our area in the 1920s and by the 1930s; all of the chestnut trees had died. Some still stood in the woods: huge, faded to white dead and others lay where they had fallen: some big enough to walk into.

The bottom, looking west from Stewart's Creek

The drawbar pasture gate on the Cleve Thomas Road was near the center of the above photo: with Grandpa's house farther up the valley toward Fisher's Peak. (Seen in the far background.) The wooded area at right was once Grandpa's pasture, his rocky cornfield was on the hilltop above and the mile-long bluff was at left.

A fur company ad promised big money by just running a trap line like they did in the Great North Woods. I was already a great hunter and with our whole country full of wild animals, I jumped on the idea with both feet.

One November day, Grandpa helped me set some of Pa's old steel traps along the creek banks. Just like the big guys up

5

north, come fair weather or foul, the great trapper was on the prowl. Even in blinding wind snow, I could hardly wait to get to the next trap to see if I'd caught anything.

Running a trap line required some wading with Pa's knee-length rubber boots and while checking a trap one cold day, a slick underwater rock caused a boot full of icy creek water.

My parents had already told me, "You're either gonna' freeze to death out there or drown down yonder in that creek." When the boot filled up, I knew I was a goner and probably "freezing to death and drowning down yonder in that creek."

I didn't know anything could be that cold and in almost no time, I got out of the creek and emptied the boot. (So much for Pa telling us boys we didn't have sense enough to pour pee out of a boot with the directions on the heel.) Everything I had shivered and when I got the boot off, the cold air felt so warm I almost cried. It was a cold trip home that never happened again.

Stewart's Creek beside the bottom

Stewart's Creek ran smooth beside Grandpa's bottom (seen above) and was a great place to wade. The left bank was once a jungle of honeysuckle vines, where muskrats pulled green cornstalks into their dens in summer. The first muskrat I caught had already drowned in the water at the Spruce Pine Hole. The second was still alive in the area of the creek seen above.

6

My storybook heroes in the Great North woods had never mentioned what to do with a live animal caught in a trap. After some pondering, self-debate, anticipation and dread, I finally drowned it with a forked stick. As was normal for most of my great projects, anticipation ran far ahead of reality. According to what I'd read, wild animals in the Great North Woods could hardly wait to jump into a steel trap, but that didn't happen on Stewart's Creek. Also, far-north trappers didn't fall in the creek, get a boot full of ice water and never had to drown an animal when they caught it. They didn't even have to take a bath.

Although not exactly overloaded with hides, I mailed away the few I had and the $12.00 check that came back was the most money I'd ever had. Being rich was a great feeling, but I'd already decided one winter on the trap line was enough to last a lifetime.

Cleve Thomas's bottom was one of the few on Stewart's Creek we never sharecropped. We *did* sharecrop Dave Carson's two smaller bottoms beyond the Thomas bottom and in fall of the year, we hauled wagonloads of corn back across the ford on Grandpa's wagon.

Pa, some of his buddies and I went 'posssum huntin' one night in the Cleve Thomas Woods. With a kerosene lantern for light and plenty of company along, I was a brave soul in the dark woods. We fought our way through blackberry briars and an ivy thicket to a tree where the dogs had treed a 'possum. Somebody aimed a flashlight along his gun barrel and shot it out of the tree; the only 'possum I ever saw on a 'possum hunt.

The High Foot Log crossed the creek between Grandpa and Cleve Thomas's bottoms. It hung high in the air, had a handrail to hang onto and planks nailed on it to walk on. It was first class, as foot logs go; it never washed away and was a great place to sit on warm summer days and watch fish swim by. It really paid for itself in winter when the creek was too cold to wade.

An August 1940 hurricane brought what became known as the "Forty Flood", the biggest ever seen on Stewart's Creek.

7

Flood water backed up almost to Grandpa's house a half-mile up the valley, all bottomland corn crops were wiped out and my whole world was a muddy mess.

The foot log that never washed away *did* that year, along with the poplar trees it was chained to. My high, dry road to everywhere that mattered was gone and it was such a disaster, I think the creek quit running until it was replaced.

The Bottoms

The Bottoms are shown above: looking from the rocky hilltop cornfield field mentioned before. The ford and the High Foot Log once crossed the creek between Grandpa's Bottom (in the foreground) and the larger Cleve Thomas Bottom (at center.) When the dam was finished, the bottoms also went under the lake.

The Cleve Thomas farm sprawled all the way from Dave Carson's Little Bottoms to the North Carolina/ Virginia state line far upstream. Cleve's hillside pasture was a so steep, it was hard to believe cows could graze on it without falling downhill. (Pa said their uphill legs were shorter than their downhill legs.)

One cold winter day, Cleve and his wife Zelphia were staying warm by the fireplace when I went by selling seeds for a school project. He bought a five-cent pack of seeds and I was on top of the world. When he died in 1943, his farm was sold and what we had always called the Cleve Thomas place became the Clyde Hayes place.

The Spruce Pine Hole

The Spruce Pine Hole was just below the High Foot Log and flowed against a large rock (seen dimly above center) and the hillside behind it was part of the mile long laurel bluff.

I caught my biggest trout at the Spruce Pine Hole and it almost got away. When I threw the line in the water, the pole bent double, I yanked the fish out of the water, it fell off the hook and I chased it all over creation.

I finally caught it just before it flopped back in the creek and since nobody had seen it happen, I could hardly wait to tell how expertly I'd landed the biggest catch of my life; it was almost as big as one that got away at the Houston Hole, the one I grieved over for days.

Dave Carson's two small bottoms were a few hundred feet below the Spruce Pine Hole: separated by a small spring branch that fell into the Abe Hole. (Named for a man named Abraham who drowned there long ago.)

A white walnut tree leaned over the hole, where most of the walnuts fell in the water and floated away. They had a great greasy taste and I grieved over such a terrible waste of good walnuts

One hot summer day, Pa and I made a fertilizer sack seine and headed for the Abe Hole. I could already taste the fish we were about to seine up and we'd probably be eating fried fish three times a day. He said we needed to start from a sandbar on the other side of the creek, because it would be easier to get in the creek from there. To avoid climbing through the tangled bluff, we waded the rough creek downstream below the Spruce Pine Hole.

As we eased into the water, he told me, "Keep quiet, move as fast as you can and keep the bottom of the seine on the bottom of the creek." As I soon found out, it's hard to keep quiet when your feet keep coming up off the creek bottom and you're about to drown: especially when you can't swim.

Judging by the few fish we caught, people could starve to death trying to live on seined fish. The few we actually caught probably died of fright from all of the thrashing and splashing. It was my only seining trip and may have been Pa's last.

On another summer day, we again headed for the Abe Hole: this time with dynamite. After the seining disaster, I'd known all along there had to be a better way to catch fish without all that seining and thrashing and drowning. Now we'd get all those that got away before and we'd probably be hauling fish home by the sled-loads. We might eat so much fried fish, we'd have to stand in the branch: the only known cure for getting foundered.

Once again we waded downstream to the same sandbar, because Pa said that was where the fish would float by after we dynamited them. He tied a piece of dynamite to a small rock, lit the fuse and threw it in the water. The dynamite came loose, floated back to the surface, exploded, scared me half to death and shook half of the county. (I'd been told to expect a small "whump.") My first thought was that a Japanese Zero had dropped one of Pa's "bums" right on top of us.

To heck with any fish, we blazed a brand new trail through the same bluff we'd avoided getting there; where no man had been before. When a neighbor later asked if we'd heard a loud explosion, we hadn't "heard nothin'."

Pa's favorite fishing place was the Big Rock Hole just below the Abe Hole. He sat on the fifteen-foot-high rock in the middle of the creek, fished, smoked roll-your-own Golden Grain cigarettes and watched the creek roll by on both sides of the rock.

When a lizard ran up his leg one day, he did an Indian war dance, came out of his pants and almost jumped off the rock. Warren and I thought it was the funniest thing we'd ever seen. When he said, "It ain't all that damn funny," it got even funnier.

Just beyond the Abe Hole, a path led up and over a small hill. Some huge beach trees stood on top, where people had carved their initials and the dates: some so long ago they were unreadable. Claude Marshall had carved his: CRM 1937 and I added mine: HWE 1940. (When the dam was built, all of the trees were bulldozed.)

The path continued downhill to the Curve Hole where the dam would later be built. A never-ending eddy of sticks and leaves circled against the far bank. I once built a campfire on a sandbar at the hole and burned some small fish on a stick that were almost edible.

Gardner's hickory trees were in a hillside across the creek, where Pa and I killed more squirrels there than at all other places combined. We sneaked in early in the morning and waited for them to come in to eat hickory nuts. Pa hunted with his .20 gauge shotgun and I hunted with my single-shot twenty-two. He said he killed the most squirrels because he threw the most lead.

I never met Linc Gardner who died in 1935, but we sharecropped his two fields on Gardner's Ridge and broke ivy in his woods: one of the few ways we had of making some extra money, sometimes our only money. Since ivy time came in late fall, it often helped Santa come to our house at Christmas.

Linc Gardner's Woods were huge and after Linc died, nobody living there for several years: making it a great country for young scouts and hunters. While running some important mission on Gardner's Ridge, I was totally absorbed in trying to figure out who and what had been there before me.

I'd read that in order to sneak up on anything, you had to go quietly, or "anything" would be long gone when you got there. I was going along quietly, with eyes wide open and rifle at ready, when a pheasant flew up almost in my face. Logic and clear thinking went out the window and I almost ran. Even first-rate trackers sometimes got surprised and after it was far too late, I finally thought about shooting the way it went.

There were other good fishing holes below the Curve Hole, but I never fished much in that area. One reason being, it was so far away and another was what happened one warm summer day while fishing near the Old Seal House.

I probably dozed off, because all of a sudden, a half dozen giggling girls were playing and splashing in the creek just around the next bend. Girls just didn't happen on my creek, but there they were, big as life, a whole pack of them. I knew right away, my creek was being invaded, something that never happened to my storybook heroes in the Great North Woods.

I made some lightning quick calculations and did the only logical thing that came to mind; I grabbed fishing pole and can of worms and headed back up the creek to God's Country. I hoped and prayed they didn't see me, because nobody needed to know I ran from a bunch of girls.

The Dam Site (Easter Sunday, April 2, 1972.)

When the photo on the previous page was made, the creek banks had already been cleared by bulldozers and construction of the dam was well under way. The Cleve Thomas Bottom was just above the top of the tower and the Curve Hole was left of the tower.

The Abe Hole and Dave Carson's little bottoms were located at the extreme right center: beyond where my dad was standing. George Easter's Bottom was located on the left side of the creek, (seen in the left background) which was about where the High Foot Log was located.

The cleared hillside at left center was once part of the mile-long laurel bluff that ended in the Tom Hawks Woods above Grandpa's house. In the far background, wind snow was falling on the Blue Ridge Mountain.

Easter Sunday, April 2,1972

From left to right above: Pa, my brother Warren, and my son Mike standing on the unfinished dam. The Cleve Thomas Woods are shown in the left background and Sugar Loaf Mountain at Lambsburg is in the extreme center background.

One dark snowy day in March 1947, my grandfather, George Washington Easter, died alone on Stewart's Creek. When he failed to come home at mid-day, Grandma went to the bottom and found him where he had died: on the creek bank beside the High Foot Log.

13

He was lying on his side with his arm under his head for a pillow, as he did when taking a nap in the floor at dinnertime. He may have fallen in the creek and froze to death, because it was a cold day and his clothes were wet. Big snowflakes kept falling, but they soon melted and someone said, "Snow don't amount to much this time of the year."

Stewart's Creek was never again like it was before and Grandma sold the home place at auction that fall and lived with her daughter Maude until she died in November 1963. That brought some huge changes in how my family lived, because we could no longer use their fields, tobacco barns and pack house.

Except for the two at the dam site, all preceding photos were made in the vicinity of the George Easter Bottom. All following photos were made going upstream from there, except the very last one: of Watershed Lake.

The Cleve Thomas Woods

Beginning in November, we broke ivy in the Cleve Thomas Woods, located across the creek from Grandpa's bottom. By that time of the year, we no longer worried about snakes, because they had already hibernated for the winter. That famous Easter theory went out the window one cold day when we met a live wide-awake copperhead while breaking ivy in Cleve's Woods.

14

Maybe it didn't get the message, or maybe it found Pa's still place and just felt too good to care. Whatever the reason, nobody got bit, but it scared us half to death. Another of our famous sayings then went down in flames and another snake never made it to hibernation.

Moonshine was the best medicine known to mankind, because it cured the mange, the croup, old age, bad news and especially snakebites. Some people drank it all year, even when snow was on the ground. As they said it, "You can't never tell and when one a' them copperheads'll git un-hibernated and come a' crawlin' back outta' the ground and bite you and you better be ready." After seeing the copperhead in November, I was a believer.

In early spring, Grandpa went into the woods and gathered an assortment of small green-all-year herbs to make what he called his herb bitters. (A spring tonic to thin winter-thickened blood) He believed anything that stayed green all winter had tremendous healing properties and according to him, "It's the best stuff I ever seen."

He mixed the herbs in a fruit jar of water, kept it cooling in the springhouse and went by every now and then for a drink. (After one drink, I knew my blood was already thin enough.)

Pa made his own blood thinner deep in the backwoods under laurel thickets. It too was powerful stuff, because he was a happy man when he drank some. According to him, "It's the best stuff I ever seen." Both he and Grandpa could drink straight from the jars without frowning, which I couldn't do.

With our ivy sacks were full, we headed for home, back across the Low Foot Log on Stewart's Creek. It was located between Oscar Marshall's bottoms and unlike the High foot Log that never washed away, the Low Foot Log did: every time the creek flooded. It had no handrail and bounced like a rubber ball when you got out in the middle.

With a good sense of balance, it was possible to get across the creek without falling in. Some people did just that and sometimes got a much-needed bath, sometimes their only one of the year, sometimes in the dead of winter.

"If you see you ain't gonna' make it across, Zeke, throw your jug in them honeysuckle vines, 'cause they ain't no use in wastin' good likker,' (Just thinking about a boot full of ice-cold creek water gave me a great sense of balance and I learned to zig when the foot log zagged.)

Stewart's Creek near the Woods Hole

The Woods Hole was a few hundred feet above Grandpa's bottom: a deep dark hole, with a huge slanted rock pointing into the woods. It looked like a good fishing hole, but I never caught the first fish there.

We once found a dead white-skinned animal about two feet long floating beside the hole. Pa said it was a water baby and since it looked so much like a baby, I didn't need to know anything else about it.

The big rock was a great place to sit on hot summer days, dangle hot feet in the cool water and watch the creek roll by. It was a different story in winter, because a high bluff blocked the low-in-the-sky sun, making the Woods Hole one of the coldest places on Stewart's Creek.

The bluff was icy and dangerous and for anyone who slipped and fell, it was a downhill slide all the way, with a creek full of ice water waiting at the bottom. The February day Mike and I were there, most of a recent snowfall was gone, but it was still slippery in the shady bluff

16

Round icicles

Round icicles had formed on twigs hanging down near the water at the Woods Hole. (Seen above.) Grandpa told about the old days when he rode his horse and wagon on the ice when Stewart's Creek froze over.

The Woods Hole area was one of the few where I saw that happen and I could almost see Grandpa riding by. I saw ice on the creek many times, but never had enough nerve to walk on it. (One boot full of icy creek water had already taught this old boy all he needed to know about such stuff and it was enough to last a lifetime.)

I could never figure out who built a long-ago campfire under a house-sized overhanging rock in Oscar Marshall's Bluff. I liked the idea that Daniel Boone could've camped there and never told anybody or maybe it was the Indians.

I thought about camping there overnight, but never quite got around to it. I'd already heard some scary crashing noises in the woods at night and even though she had died many years ago, Old Blind Topsy was said to still be out there.

She could cast spells, remove warts, cause milk to curdle, (in the cow) do other weird things and still "got" somebody now and then. Nobody really believed all that stuff, but I did wonder how fast a blind person could run.

17

Mike at the rainy-day shelter

Beyond a doubt, I could out-run anything that got after me, unless something got in my way. The only problem with that: with so many trees, blackberry briars and honeysuckle thickets in the way, it would've been be a hard scary run back home in the dark. Needless to say, I never camped there alone at night.

The rock was a great rainy day shelter, but I built no campfires there, because Pa had already warned me what would happen if I caused a wildfire. "Boy, you set them woods a' fire and I'll set *your* woods a' fire." That brought an end to any thoughts of building a campfire anywhere except where there was plenty of water to douse it.

After sweating all day in the hot summer fields, nothing beat a good swim in the Swimming Hole. It was one of the highlights of summer and every chance we got, we headed for Stewart's Creek.

Since time began, people in our world went swimming in their birthday suits. Nobody I knew had ever owned or even seen a swimsuit and anybody goofy enough to wear one would've been laughed out of the county.

The Swimming Hole was a few hundred yards above the Woods Hole: one of the deeper holes on Stewart's Creek. It was a fair place to fish, but with a big rock to dive from, it was a better place to swim.

18

Mike and Dad at the Swimming Hole

Pa and I never learned to swim, but we jumped off the big rock and did some big-time splashing every chance we got. Those happy times came to an end one day when he suggested we go for another swim. Things had changed since the last time and certain signs of growing up were showing up in certain places on me.

Such earth-shaking events as the facts of life were *never* discussed in our family, but I'd already learned that our new calf didn't really come from a hollow log like I'd been told and rather than be embarrassed, I sneaked Pa's razor and did some shaving. It was our last swim together.

One Sunday afternoon, Mama, some of her friends and us kids were returning home after a visit to a neighbor's house near Stewart's Creek. I ran on ahead and overtook two neighborhood girls who had been swimming at the Swimming Hole and were also on their way home.

They accused me of being down at the Swimming Hole watching them swim. Of course I hadn't and when Mama and the others caught up with us, they finally believed me. I wasn't about to ask, but I did wonder if they wore their birthday suits when they went swimming.

Someone told about Pa seeing some girls swimming in the Swimming Hole when he was growing up. They also wore their

19

birthday suits and Pa didn't run like somebody else did down at the old Seal House. (I never got up enough nerve to ask him about that.)

The Lower Hole

The Lower Hole was just above the Swimming Hole: located in a bend of the creek between Oscar Marshall's two bottoms. When the air was right, I could hear the rapids (seen above) from our house: singing me a fishing song. It was my favorite fishing hole on all of Stewart's Creek and when a summer thunderstorm ran the creek muddy that was where I headed, because catfish would then bite everything but an empty hook.

Time stood still in the alder bush shade, as I watched the creek roll by on its way to an ocean "way down yonder somewhere." I dreamed up many great backwoods missions, while black walnuts grew on a tree across the creek.

With rifle, telescope, fishing pole, can of worms and the best fishing hole known to mankind, what else could anybody need? Sadly, a thunderstorm or suppertime brought many great adventures to an end, but another day was coming tomorrow and I planned to be there.

During the Big War, I dreamed a huge gray Navy battleship had dropped anchor in the Lower Hole. It was as tall as the surrounding hills and had gone up-stream as far as it could go. I knew in the dream that someone had done a great job bringing it that far from the ocean. What my dream didn't realize was how much water was needed for a ship that size. (After the dam was finished, there was enough there to float it.)

Oscar's Big Bottom, with Sugar Loaf Mountain
at back

When the above photo was made, Oscar's Big Bottom had not been farmed for many years and had grown up in broom straw and small pine trees. It was on the west side of the creek beside the Lower Hole.

We sharecropped both of Oscar's bottoms in the early years and in the middle of summer, they were "the hottest places I ever seen." Just like at Grandpa's bottom, there was no time to wade the creek on hoeing day. As Pa said it, "Gotta' hoe that corn while the sun shines, boys." At least the dirt was soft, easy to work and I found Indian arrowheads in the dirt when Pa plowed up new dirt.

The big bottom was shaped like a flat-bottomed bowl: with a high hill on the west side that was a lifesaver on corn hoeing days, because it caused the sun to go down earlier than it did on the high ridges. When working in the high ridge fields, there were times when I thought the days would never end. They always did when the sun went behind the mountain, then we got a night's rest and did it all over again next day.

Pa once set up his still in a bluff beside the Big Bottom. Armed with slingshot and some small rocks, I kept watch from the hilltop. I had no idea what a lawman looked like, but from what I'd heard, they were big, bad, ugly and had horns and I was supposed to yell and run if I saw one.

The law population was never in any danger from me, but it could've been a different story with Pa, because he kept "Old Betsy" handy: ready to shoot and run, but it never happened.

The "biggest pine tree in the country" stood on a ridge above the bottoms and could be seen from "everywhere n' half a' Georgia," as Pa said it. (In later years, the Marshall family hired Robert Earl East to saw it down; then nobody could find their way home.)

The Low Foot Log was at a ford between Oscar's two bottoms. It was shaky, unsteady and it hated people, especially in winter when the creek water was coldest. With a good sense of balance, it was possible to get to the other side without falling in the creek. In summer, kids didn't worry about foot logs, they just dived in and waded across. "You all stay out of them honeysuckle vines, because they's all kinds of varmints in there just waitin' to eat you alive."

Since our sled went under water when hauling fertilizer across the ford, we used Grandpa's wagon and in fall of the year, we used it again to haul corn, corn tops and fodder *back* across the creek.

A road led through Oscar's Big Bottom, down to the ford and ended there. It had once continued through the Little Bottom and uphill through the Cleve Thomas Woods and to a rail fence at Cleve's spring. (That was the road I traveled when he bought the packet of seeds.)

One late August day, we were cutting corn tops in the Big Bottom and took a break in the shade of an apple tree. Dog days had already gone back down south where they belonged and it felt good to flop back in the cool grass and watch whippoorwills fly around overhead. They flew back and forth in every direction all over the sky: headed south for the winter, with no apparent sense of where south was.

A dilapidated log barn stood near the bottom, but it had no door and was no longer used. We were told, "You all stay out of there, 'cause they's copperheads, blue tailed scorpions, black widders' and no tellin' what else in there." Like so many other dangers we were warned of, I was almost afraid to look at it.

The Old House

John Coalson built the above log cabin about 1880, on a small knoll beside Stewart's Creek and many different people had called it home over the years: including Sam Coalson who lived there in the late 1930s.

He had snow-white hair, a long white beard and looked a lot like Santa Clause as he baked corn bread in a black iron skillet in the fireplace. He frightened me out of my wits when he explained the shotgun hole in the front door.

Someone had tried to kill John Coalson while he lived there and Sam said he could look through the hole and see who was out there. I was almost afraid to look: afraid somebody might shoot again: right through the same hole, right into my eye.

When Mike and I were there that February day, Oscar and Lillie Marshall and family owned the house, the ninety-five acres of land around it and had once lived there. After they moved away, they called it the "Old House at the Old Place."

The white oak roof shingles had curled up because they were made in the wrong moon sign. The doorstep was a big creek rock and the four corners of the house were supported by more of them. Like most log cabins, the spaces between the logs were daubed with red mud and most of it had fallen out, leaving air holes.

The inside walls were covered with newspaper and magazine pages: glued there with flour paste to keep out the winter wind. There was still no shortage of cold inside, but with a stack of quilts on the bed and a roaring fire in the fireplace, it was possible to stay alive, even in the middle of winter.

Some older log cabins had no windows, but had shutters that could be opened and closed according to the weather. With a window in the east wall, the Old House was right up to date. Word had it that log cabins would last for a hundred years, maybe a lifetime if you died when you ought to. The Old House almost made it!

Sam Coalson was a lucky man; he carried water downhill from his spring in a hollow above the house, instead of uphill as we did. Using an old well in the front yard would have made more sense, but it was covered with rotten planks and was never used. We were warned to stay away from it: one of the few times we did exactly as we were told.

A footpath led uphill through a pasture, passed the spring and continued to the Graveyard Road on top of the hill. A few people who once lived in the Old House were buried there in a small cemetery. By the 1940s, huge trees had grown up among the graves and the whole area had almost completely returned to the forest.

There were no names or dates on the sand rock headstones, but following tradition, the people were buried with their heads to the west: assuring the sun will shine in their faces when they rise up on Resurrection Morning.

The Graveyard Road continued south and joined our road. (Later named Banjo Lane) Turning *right* on our road, led by our house and on to Lambsburg Road at the foot of Jim's Knob. Turning *left* on our road led back to the Old House where the road passed very close to the chimney.

Beyond the chimney, the road crossed the spring branch and continued upstream beside Stewart's Creek. It was dug out of the hillside many years ago and at one time, according to my parents, it was well used by wagons, horseback riders and an occasional "T" Model.

It was no longer a highway when I was growing up and had almost completely grown up in blackberry and honeysuckle vines. Except for a few horseback riders and people on foot, I saw no traffic there and it was like having my own private highway to the great fishing holes upstream. (That part of the road also went under the lake.)

Looking back at the Big Bottom from the road

The road continued upstream by a barbed wire fence that turned straight uphill toward the Graveyard Road. What had once been a pasture had gone back to the forest and the trees that were used for fence posts had grown so much, the rusty wire was in the center of the trunks.

25

The icy creek upstream from the Old House

The Upper Hole

The road ran close to the Upper Hole at a bend in the creek: so close, you could sit in the road and fish. A spring branch, formed by the four springs of Oscar Marshall, Sid Marshall, Farley and Jim Smith fell into the creek beside the hole. The road then led into the woods by the Kettle Spring.

The name came into being when someone installed an enamel kettle in the spring for a reservoir. Everybody who came by drank water from the fancy spring with an enamel dipper that hung on a bush. Fancy spring water was much better than ordinary water and just like every other spring I ever heard of, the Kettle Spring had "the coldest water in the whole country."

Rotten planks, a jumble of rocks and a rusted-out steel barrel were all that remained of an old still place hidden under a nearby laurel thicket. It was said people who ran stills were preparing for hard times. There must have been an epidemic of hard times in other years, because I found old still places along almost all of the backwoods streams.

Dad on top of the small hill

The main road continued to Houston's house on top of the hill at the North Carolina/Virginia state line. A path across from the spring turned right and bypassed a rough section of the creek, then led over a small hill to the Houston Thomas Bottom

The Houston Hole was beside Houston's Bottom: the fastest, deepest, roughest fishing hole on Stewart's Creek. To get to it, you had to slide down a ten-foot sandy bank and to get back up into the bottom you had to claw, dig and scratch.

I hooked the biggest trout of all time at the Houston Hole and when it bit, I jerked it out of the water, it shook a couple of times, came off the hook and fell back in. I thought about jumping in after it, but even I knew the water was much too deep and fast.

Mike at the Houston Hole

The first thing that came to mind was the old saying, "You should've seen the one that got away." I fished there many other times, hoping it would bite again, but it never did.

By late winter, everyday meals of pinto beans, corn bread and fatback were getting tiresome and we craved something new, fresh and green to eat. That was when thoughts turned to creecies.

They were low-on-the-ground green plants that lazed along all winter. Along about February, they began growing and every family I knew headed for last-year's cornfields to gather a mess. We then had pinto beans, corn bread, fatback and *creecies to eat*

Creecies grew well in Houston's bottom: one of the few cornfields we didn't sharecrop on Stewart's Creek. If it had been available, no doubt about it, we'd have been there, digging and plowing, just like we did in every other field Pa could find. In fall of the year, we gathered black walnuts from a huge tree in the middle of the field.

I don't remember Houston Thomas, who died in 1935, but he cut our hair in the early years at his white frame house on top of the hill. With a nice feed barn and a corral made of planks, the place looked like what I thought a ranch would look like; all it needed was a bunkhouse, some horses, a chuck wagon and a few cowboys.

The Houston House

After Houston died, his wife Zora married Virgil Harrison, who once lived "out west" and owned a room-sized tent he set up beside yard. He never knew how I envied him having a tent to sleep in and I would've traded everything I owned, which wasn't much, to set it up down at the Abe Hole.

One summer night, Avon and Russell Marshall, my brother Warren and I made a fishing-by-lantern-light expedition along Houston's Bottom. We had planned it for days and on the big night, we fought black berry briars and mosquitoes along the creek banks, chased each other in the dark and finally caught a few small catfish.

We had no watch, but with all of our vast experience, we decided it was bedtime and climbed up the hill to the Houston Thomas house.

Nobody lived there at that time and we had decided to camp there and sleep on the back porch where snakes couldn't get us. Sometime in the wee hours of the morning, we went to sleep with visions of a big breakfast in the great outdoors.

After a good night's sleep, everybody woke up at the same time and again, pooling our vast experience, we agreed the sky was getting brighter, which meant daylight was coming.

We built a campfire in the side-yard, boiled coffee in a tin can and burned our fish on sticks over the fire. With warmed-over wheat bread from home and some fried fatback, it was the best breakfast ever.

The eastern sky was still no brighter, which seemed odd. Since we'd already had a good night's sleep, were well fed and wide-awake, we headed for home. Surely the sun would be up by the time we walked the long way back through Virginia.

When we finally got to Bate's Hill on Lambsburg Road, it was still dark and we were getting worried. Something had gone badly wrong somewhere, because we hadn't seen the sun for at least a week. Maybe it forgot to come up. What if it never came up again? What if the lantern ran out of kerosene oil? I'd already heard some scary crashing noises in the woods at night and being out there with no light was the last thing I needed.

We continued up Bate's Hill and finally, at long last, we met a foxhunter at the North Carolina-Virginia state line. (It was a great relief to know other people were still alive in the world.) Using only his pocket-watch, he solved all of our problems; it was 2:00 in the morning. That was our first and last camping trip on Stewart's Creek.

When Mike and I finally made it to Houston's Bottom that February day, we were tired, cold, hungry and didn't go any farther upstream. Since the Line Hole would not be going under water, we decided to wait for another day. (As it came to be it was many years later.)

The North Carolina/Virginia state line crossed the creek at the Line Hole, at the tallest trees seen in the background of the photo on the following page. I liked the idea of sitting in one state and fishing in another.

A barbed wire fence crossed the creek at the Line Hole: with a broken post still attached. Leaves had gathered around the post and when the water flowed under it, it bounced up out of the water, then fell back in; making a continual splashing sound. (A few days later, the post was gone.)

I remember sitting at the Line Hole in the warm spring sunshine. Maple trees were blooming, grass was growing, birds were singing and after a long cold winter, it felt good to sit there and soak up the sunshine.

An icy Houston Thomas Bottom

The Line Hole (2009)

When the Line Hole photo was made some thirty-eight years later, it looked nothing like I remembered.

The last photo made that day became my last look at the
Stewart's Creek I grew up with.

Watershed Lake at the George Easter home place (2002)

Never again will spring come to the Stewart's Creek I grew up with. Never again will the bottoms be spring-plowed, nor will corn ever again grow tall enough to touch the sky. No more gold will be panned in the sandbars, nor will anyone ever again go skinny-dipping in the Swimming Hole, seine the Abe Hole, or sit in a certain look-out tree high in the bluff and watch the world go by down below.

Even though they can no longer be seen, every single one of those places is still there in memory, buried deep under Watershed Lake. Maybe just maybe, when nobody expects it, when the air is just right, Stewart's Creek will once again sing me a fishing song as it falls down over the rapids at the Lower Hole and maybe, just maybe, spring will come again to the only river I ever knew, my river of childhood that was once such a great part of my life.

Made in the USA
Middletown, DE
28 December 2023